THE **PILLARS**
OF **TRUST**

A Comprehensive Guide to empower
you in your Self-Trust journey.

NANCY ANDINO, LCSW, CASAC

Author: Nancy Andino, LCSW, CASAC

Illustrations: Doan Trang L

For accompanying online course visit our website
www.Tailoredforchange.com

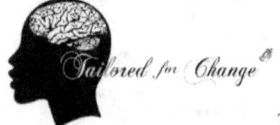

TM

TABLE OF CONTENTS

WELCOME

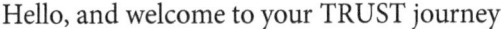

Hello, and welcome to your TRUST journey

Trust is an emotional and physical experience. We feel then think. This process may not always be clear. Particularly when negative emotions and experiences that may have been traumatizing, disturbing, annoying, or just not right! weaken your rational thinking muscles, causing your emotional flexibility to become stiff and restrictive. Your beliefs, expectations, boundaries and self-trust gets impacted. To trust others, you have to be right from within. You need to have clarity about your boundaries, values and trust in your ability to honor them. What happens if you allow yourself to do what is right for you? Can you trust your ability to manage the emotions, sensations and thoughts that will present themselves? Can you cope with the emotions or will you numb the sensations? Are you willing to feel your feels as you practice trusting you with the understanding that failure is a possibility?

I welcome you to your self-TRUST journey.

The intention of this workbook is for you to easily refer to it; with the understanding that it may turn out to be an emotional rollercoaster, with a ride that challenges your beliefs, expectations and the relationship with yourself. I am not here to uproot your life, but to disrupt it in a meaningful way. The focus will be on your ability to trust yourself, and to prioritize honoring you first and foremost, before trusting others including me.

The motivation behind this workbook came from the wellness retreat, " The PILLARS of TRUST" that I created, hosted and facilitated; leading me to create an organic curriculum. The prompts in this workbook are based on client, family, cultural, retreats and professional interactions. All these exercises are a result of my curiosity, desire for learning and assisting others in their wellness journeys, along with the needs and challenges witnessed as a mental health professional. I challenge, question, explore, poke, reflect, mirror, role play, and improvise with clients. I do all of this with love, self-trust, curiosity and their guidance. I have learned important skills in the room. I believe the partnerships with clients are healthy, intentional, driven, and impactful. I trust the holistic step by step journey. If I forget or miss something during a session, I take ownership and make sure to start the follow-up session with the message I've received or the awareness I've gained. In my journey of trust, I've learned to be tender, self-compassionate and trust that what I know and share with clients is the best I can offer at that time. I continue to learn, explore, and be curious about new techniques, modalities, and skills as I approach my 25-year mark in this field.

My clients have found me and have chosen to work with me because I look like them, the tone of my voice, my accent reminds them of home, or someone they know, or a family member. My skin color makes them feel comfortable because they understand that we may have had very similar experiences, my hair reminds them of the challenges they may experience with their hair. My immigrant background helps them feel safe and able to speak freely in their spoken language; my dialect, ability to be transparent, a mixture of laymen's terms with professional gibberish and "urban" terminology, allows them to trust that the work we will be doing together, will be meaningful, challenging, loving, trustworthy and life changing. They learn about the trainings I take. I share what I find helpful and not helpful. I suggest things for them to try and experiment with. They have learned to trust me with themselves during the most vulnerable and rawest times, and that is why I work on honoring my boundaries and solidifying TRUST within me, which allows me to guide and assist in their trust journey, so they can trust themselves the same way they have trusted me. This has allowed me to create and share this workbook with you.

In order to complete this workbook, you will need:

- Vulnerability
- Courage
- Willingness to feel uncomfortable
- Willingness to practice
- Patience
- Permission
- Permission to speak to yourself aloud
- A journal/ diary/ notebook if you have the electronic version of this book
- Crayons, Color pencils
- Pen
- YOU

This workbook is NOT to be used as an alternative to therapy, if things get too emotionally sticky for you, I recommend you seek support from a mental health professional.

If you have not mastered the basics of trusting yourself, but have mastered your defenses most of your life; I ask that you borrow from those survival warrior skills that have protected you in this world and have your trust thus far. Utilize the skills, energy and dedication that you've used as protection, to assist you with experiencing your emotions, fears, disappointments, joys, and love, to teach you to trust you.

Let's start with these basic steps, where the need for consistency can become a major challenge;

> Give yourself permission to drink water when your body asks for it.
>
> Use the restroom when you feel the need to, even if it's interrupting a conversation, or stopping a workflow.
>
> Stretch when your body asks you for it.
>
> Sleep, because you're lying to yourself if you believe you can live a healthy life with just 4-5 hours of sleep at night. And if you can't sleep, get to figuring out the why, and seek support.

You trust your body to take care of you and to function, when it's riddled with stress, when it has pulled and torn muscles and tendons; trusting that even with knee pains, ankle pains, back pains, dry eyes, and carpal tunnel, that it can still get you through one more day of working and showing up for others. However, when it comes to listening to yourself, to taking care of your body's needs, emotional responses, fears, and gut feeling, it can become impossible to respond to it. The small voice that communicates the truth, gets overshadowed by the need for others' permission to be you. The overachieving, "I'm strong and confident" mask; the numbing, avoiding, and ignoring that takes place, causes you to fake like you're present, while abandoning yourself. Instead of trusting you, you rely on what others say you should do, and what they've decided is the norm. You base your life's principles and values on what fearful people or those focused on others say. Perhaps the fear of accountability, making mistakes, not being liked, judged, or being perceived as an a %$^* , prevents you from trusting your own experiences and responding accordingly.

Be curious and explore, question and challenge your behaviors and beliefs. Learn to trust that you have the right to try something new, even if it goes against what people in your network are doing or believing. You are able to practice managing your emotions and sensations, particularly because you have survived and lived through hard, challenging, difficult, uncomfortable times.

Acknowledge and understand that you will make mistakes and experience feelings of fear, annoyance, impatience and even cursing me and everyone else out, because of the discomfort you will experience. TRUST will ask for you to practice Letting GO!! Letting go of your expectations, letting go of the fears, and getting in the driver seat. This is a process of loss and gains. You will practice listening and choosing your identity, thoughts, and feelings. You will challenge relationships and others' expectations. You reassess the roles you've played in these relationships, which can result in loss. Remember, your body will continue to wrestle, kick, and push you, until you listen to it, and if you don't, it'll break you down until you do. So might as well give yourself the permission to practice trusting you, as you learn to build a supportive community and gain the trust within you.

I recommend you Buckle up! because this workbook on trust will mess you up, in a good way.

Not much fluff talk will take place, whatever I see that needs additional information I will expand on. You know your story and your behaviors. I will ask for you to stop hiding from yourself and to expand your tolerance level of vulnerability, discomfort and honesty. Feel! get more curious with what you're experiencing. I will try to make it as least scary as I can; and in your expansion process you will need to allow yourself to get muddy, to experience disgust, shame, guilt, anger, fear, relief, love, and joy, which will lead you to feeling free.

I ask that you give yourself permission to explore and understand your definition of trusting yourself. Your ability to trust yourself does not only depend on your lived experiences, it depends on your parents and their parents' lived experiences, and their parents, parents lived experiences, and on and on. If you have picked up this workbook you may have some awareness of generational pass downs, such as customs, traditions, clothing, recipes, traumas, and being able to trust yourself; it is all on the same thread. We are raised through the lens of our parents, that's why we have certain nuances, behaviors, sayings, the way we walk, talk, respond to situations and the way we respond in this world; we were molded from the moment we entered this world.

You may ask, what grants me the opportunity and privilege to create this workbook. Well, I am a Licensed Clinical Social Worker, trained in multiple therapeutic modalities, and I bring something from all of them including me. I will draw from my professional training, mental health expertise, and personal experiences to guide you in this book. I've been certified in the following;

- Substance abuse and addiction
- Gestalt Therapy
- Cognitive Behavioral Therapy
- Eye Movement Desensitization and Reprocessing
- Trauma Therapy
- The Daring Way
- Reiki
- Breath work
- My life

These modalities complement one another, and they complement who I am as a person. I'm caring, challenging, in your face, loud, transparent, loving, affectionate, inquisitive, stubborn, supportive and a student of life.

Some brief information about me, so you can get an idea of where my head is at, where my experiences and beliefs come from, and what has allowed me to put this together.

The challenges I witnessed, the images I saw and the desire to want to help, motivated me to embark on the social services, mental health professional journey. I made the decision to assist, help, support, and challenge people who experienced substance abuse at the age of 14, when I was asked what I wanted to do by my very religious aunt. I understood hurt people's desire and need to numb from an early age, I don't really know how or why, but I just did; it made sense to me. I started my professional journey as an Alcoholism and Substance Abuse Counselor, because of what I witnessed in my family, neighborhood, and the schools I attended. The strength, capacity and trust that it takes to be able to learn to cope with feelings, to experience discomforts, to remember and relive traumatic and disturbing memories without numbing, is a high ask. How can we expect people to do well and be able to "emotionally function" ? when no one has taken the time to teach it or to be the compass that can assist people to cope with life challenges. The experience as an addiction's counselor led me to start graduate school.

I graduated with my Masters in Social Work from the Wurzweiler School of Social Work, at Yeshiva University. A few months after graduation, I took my licensing exam. I started working at a community counseling center, providing therapy services. A couple of jobs later, I noticed a desire to want to do more, to "have more of an impact" as an administrator, but most importantly I wanted to continue sharpening my skills in the therapeutic space. I was working as an administrator and still providing therapy services to the community in the evenings.

By "chance" I became interested in Gestalt therapy, which I had never heard of (maybe I fell asleep in class during the 5 minutes it may have been discussed in the master's program). I typed in Google search, "therapies that allow clients to experience, learn and listen to their emotions." What I was witnessing with clients who experienced anxiety, depression, feeling stuck, avoidant, addicted, having unhealthy behaviors and other life changing experiences, I knew talk therapy was going to get them nowhere. Gestalt came up in the search. I called the program and within 3 months I was in this post graduate expensive $#% program.

During the Gestalt program journey, it allowed me to step into another room of white people, as the only Puerto Rican in my class with an Afro at the time. I walked in with my knee-high boots, fitted pants, lip gloss, a Puerto Rican New York accent and masterful defenses. These defenses started in the island of Puerto Rico, where teachers were allowed to hit you - THE NERVE!, (my Mami was not having any of that) and sharpened in the Brooklyn, NY neighborhoods of Red Hook and Fort Greene Projects (Public housing).

Fortunately, I was raised by a mom that allowed me to speak up and honor my NO, choose the clothes I wanted to wear from like the age of 4, that was very important (everything was yellow during my primary school years, LOL). Needless to say, I felt secure to express myself and to honor my boundaries, my defenses got sharper as I got older.

In the becoming a Gestalt therapist journey, I learned how my body is constantly communicating, that it needs to be heard, acknowledged and given a voice; where visualization can unlock the darkest and brightest parts of us. (In Gestalt, when we talk about parts, we mean each of us has various aspects of our personality that interact and affect our relationships with ourselves and others. But the most crucial impact is on ourselves. These parts evolve based on lived experiences; for example, the part of us that is childish, the polish part, the professional part, the loving part, the rebellious part, the defender, etc.) I learned to trust that the defensive parts of me had a voice and a purpose, and learned how to utilize them, not how to shut them, shame or avoid them. These defenses were my creative adjustments. Creative adjustments automatically take place, helping your functioning in challenging spaces. Your brain adapts to survive, connect, and to navigate life. Your brain will always try to adjust to new situations.

Then I added Eye Movement Desensitization and Reprocessing training, another all white people space, where vulnerability and reliving of traumatic experiences is a necessity in order for the therapy to work; if I didn't allow myself to be vulnerable in the room, then I wouldn't be able to witness my client's experiences and/or guide and assist them in the therapy room; I would not be able to support and help them desensitize the traumatic memories that are causing them to not be able to trust themselves, to drown in their emotions, to experience anxiety, depression, panic disorders, obsessions, and addictions.

Then the Daring Way certification program, based on the research of Dr. Brené Brown, another room of let's be generous, 98% white people, mainly white women. Here I owned aaaalllll of me, with the support of my Mami. I remember the first day of training in 2019, going back to my hotel room in Texas during the lunch break, and my Mami was getting ready to head out, to explore the town and have her lunch, I told her, "Mami, aqui lo que hay es un monton de mujeres blancas, nadamas vi como 5 personas de color.

Como siempre" and her response to me was "Tu pagaste lo mismo que esa gente blanca, aprovechate Y aprende, tu tienes el mismo derecho y sabiduria que ellos". That was all I needed, confirmation from my mom that I was worthy and was just as smart and paid my money just like everyone else in the room. I practiced being courageous and vulnerable by stating my intention, my purpose for putting myself in the room and giving myself permission to not try to protect the white people from their feelings and responses to what I would express, experience and share in the room as my true lived experience. My vulnerability in a program focused on vulnerability and shame looked different from theirs, but very similar emotions, with the caveat that in the US they are able to fully own and express theirs, but in my US experience it's dangerous and threatening for me to express it. I still gave myself permission to OWN and trust my voice, to trust myself in the process and to make connections with the handful of other people of color in the room, with no fear of how I would be judged or looked at by my white professional peers.

Then I moved on to breath and body work, which I sew into these modalities. My ability to practice trusting myself was a necessity that allowed me to practice mastering my skills, living my human life and the continuation of being curious, challenging, bold, outspoken, and open to learning, as I practiced trusting myself every step of the way.

PERMISSION TO BE VULNERABLE

We start your trust journey with permission. In the Daring Way, we start all of our sessions with giving ourselves permission. It can be permission to be present, to be uncomfortable, to feel your emotions; whatever you have chosen to notice and want to allow yourself to experience, that can grant you the ability to welcome and understand the information and journey you are choosing. As you identify the permission you will be giving yourself throughout this journey, be assured that it is based on your needs in this very moment, based on what led you to choose this workbook. Identify the steps that you will take to honor and to hold yourself accountable.

I give myself permission to _____
and the way that I will practice honoring it will be by
_____.   If   and
when I notice that I am straying away from the permission
that I have given myself, I will do the following;

_____

_____

_____

_____

_____

Throughout this workbook you will experience an array of
emotions, as you practice applying the exercises, and building the skills needed to build trust with yourself. The emotional discomforts you will experience can show up with
feelings of anger, grief, fear, loss, relief, anxiety, depression,
disbelief, shame, harshness, etc. Vulnerability to experience
these emotions is needed to allow yourself to be compassionate and kind to how you are responding. Let's remember, this was not practiced growing up, and what you may
have witnessed as it relates to trust may have looked like dis-
appointment, co-dependency, not trusting other's ability to
follow through, trusting that they would respond in a manner that was not positive, trusting that you or a loved one

would be taken advantage of; all of which distorts your views and how you learn to have trust in yourself and others. You are doing something new, something that you have not witnessed. In the Daring Way, vulnerability is taught from a lens of being vulnerable with others and practicing allowing yourself to be seen and to experience the unknown.

When working with clients in the therapy room, I view and utilize vulnerability in a slightly different manner, particularly when my clients look like me. I cannot ask a client to allow themselves to be vulnerable in a world where people of color are not safe to be vulnerable in. Trauma is imbedded in our blood, passed down through generations, and it manifests as heightened survival skills. Vulnerability is a privilege that not many people get to practice and experience. The struggle to trust themselves with their emotions and body sensations based on the lived experiences, create an incredible defensive barrier, and a fear or hesitation of not being able to cope with the emotions. The worry of expressing themselves and facing consequences like getting fired or hurt hinders the trust process.

Vulnerability will be practiced with others who are worthy of receiving it, this aligns perfectly with vulnerability in the Daring Way. We need to first make sure that you are able to be vulnerable to experience the emotions that will show up for you in this journey; to trust your ability to manage emotions that you have been trained to not experience or believe in; to experience the emotions that cannot be expressed because it can be costly in many different ways, and to practice feeling. Vulnerability is a necessity, mindfulness is a necessity, awareness is a necessity, compassion is a necessity, in order to TRUST oneself. When teaching trust to my clients, vulnerability is first in line and it looks and sounds something like this.

Using Dr. Brené Brown's definition of vulnerability in the book Daring Greatly:

"Vulnerability is uncertainty, risk, and emotional exposure". (2012 P. 34)

Yes, I am asking you to allow yourself to be vulnerable, but first with yourself. The risk you will experience is discomfort, you will feel emotions you do not want to experience, such as anxiety, depression, loneliness, sadness, grief, but if you purchased this workbook is because a part of you is telling you, that you are ready to practice trusting yourself, you are tired of needing to talk to everyone and their momma before making a decision. You are tired of questioning every single aspect of yourself, and going through every single what if, until you basically get sick to your stomach or become so overwhelmed, that you choose to not take action, or just say F%$# it, whatever happens will happen. And when the whatever happens, happen you end up unable to experience self-trust. This lack of self-trust impacts your coping skills and their ability to catch you and help you manage during difficult times.

According to Iyanla Vanzant in her book TRUST, she shares vulnerability being an

"Archenemy of the negative ego". " The negative ego hates change because it engenders fears. Consequently, as you begin to change your thoughts, beliefs, and reactions to the physical

world, the negative ego will fight you". " It does not want to change, and it is certainly not willing to trust anything or anyone, including you! Why? Because it knows that any changes you make for the better will cause it's death". (2015 P. 15)

That's what's being asked of you in this workbook, to change and decimate the negative self-talk, insecurities, and anxieties in order to trust yourself.

The prompts in this workbook, are to be used just as that, as a prompt; how I phrase things and my style of writing may be different from yours, give yourself permission to describe, answer the questions and finish the prompts in whatever way feels most organic to you, while still doing the work and not censoring yourself.

Let's begin

Define vulnerability in your own words; in the manner that you experience and digest it; it does not have to be the way it was defined. Allow yourself to have a natural response to vulnerability, no censoring or numbing of sensations.

Vulnerability to me means _____

_____

_____

As you think about vulnerability, what images, memories, sensations are showing up for you in this moment? Draw it and welcome your inner artist with no judgment

Did you allow yourself to draw? ___ Yes ____ No why?

_____

_____

_____

Are you ok with the experience that you are having in this moment? __Yes ___ No describe _____

_____

_____

_____

Recognizing your feelings and understanding vulnerability, is the first step to embracing vulnerability in the future. As you complete the workbook exercise, allow yourself to be as vulnerable as you can tolerate, and when you feel it's been enough, I want you to ask yourself;

Am I ok with this level of not knowing? _____

Am I ok with this level of discomfort? _____, let's be curious and ask; why, and what do I want to do about it? _____

_____

_____

_____

Here are questions to spark your curiosity in any vulnerable situation. These prompts can be helpful for practicing.

- What about this situation/ feeling, is making me feel comfortable or uncomfortable?
- What am I telling myself?
- Is what I'm telling myself real or is it made up?
- Does this narrative support what I need? how?
- What steps do I give myself permission to take?

Draw what you're feeling, experiencing, seeing;

A few clarifying points;

- The simple act of you drawing like no one is critiquing you, is being vulnerable.

- Not censoring your experience and verbalizing what you're thinking is part of being vulnerable. Allowing yourself to experience emotions without punishing yourself for having them, is being vulnerable.

- Acknowledging the sensation of a vibration coming up or down your spine, or your stomach doing flips because you are acknowledging and understanding the emotions you are experiencing to yourself, is being vulnerable.

- Admitting that you are feeling anxious, experiencing depression, not being able to focus or respond in a manner you feel you should be able to, is being vulnerable with yourself.

It may feel like I'm giving you a lot of points here, but in order to trust yourself, we need to acknowledge the "Basics" of you being human and experiencing the emotions and sensations that accompany the human experience.

I can allow myself to be vulnerable with the following emotions and in these situations;

1. _____

   _____

2. _____

   _____

3. _____

   _____

The reason why I am able to be vulnerable with these emotions in these situations is because

_____

_____ and it allows me to

_____

and I can utilize these examples as a steppingstone to allow me to _____

_____

_____

as I begin to trust my ability to experience me.

After this quick introduction to vulnerability, you can now observe your experiences and reactions. This shows that you are practicing mindfulness. The infamous mindfulness…

THE IMPACT OF MINDFULNESS

Mindfulness is noticing what you're feeling; your body sensations, your breathing patterns, the way your brain tries to interrupt with random thoughts and lists to keep you feeling busy and productive. It's noticing the space you take up and how you show up. Mindful about your decision making, your emotions, the people you allow in your life, the jobs you accept and the reason why you accept them; the way people speak with you, to you or at you and how you cope with it. Mindfulness in how you refer to yourself and how you treat yourself, such as noticing the cadence in your voice, the thoughts that show up, the sensations being experienced. In order to trust yourself, mindfulness is a necessity.

Let's do a quick mindfulness exercise:

As you are reading and writing on this workbook, or pdf or on your journal, I want you to pause and follow this exercise and notice what your body is experiencing.

Breathe in through your nose 1, 2,3, 4 and out through your nose 1, 2, 3, 4 , try to maintain this breathing rhythm and once you notice you're calm, slowly return to your natural breathing pattern.

Breathe in through your nose 1, 2,3, 4 and out through your nose 1, 2, 3, 4

Notice your jaw; does it feel tense? are you clenching your jaw and your teeth? do you need to loosen it up? if so, loosen it up. Notice the sensation.

Notice your throat, does it feel dry? do you need water? if you do, drink water.

Notice the sensation.

Notice your eyes, are you squinting at the screen? is the font too small for you? do your eyes burn? do your eyes feel tired because you've been in front of a screen for several hours today? do you need to put eye drops in your eyes? if you do, please get up and put eye drops in your eyes.

Notice the sensation

Notice your neck and shoulders, are they feeling tension? are you hunched over? are you feeling the sensation and desire to have to put your hands on your neck and put pressure on your neck to see if it gives you relief? Do it and notice the sensation.

Notice your wrist and hands, do they hurt? do they need to be stretched because you've been typing or grabbing and picking things up all day? Do you need to clench your fingers into a fist? if so, do so and release.

Notice the sensation.

Notice your chest, are you experiencing tension and/or pressure? does it feel like an elephant is sitting on your chest? If so, breathe and open up your chest, open and close your arms, switch your breathing patterns, loosen up until you experience relief.

Notice the sensation.

Notice your belly, is it asking you for food with its loud growling? does your belly feel tension because you have been holding in your stomach all day? Loosen your belly, unbutton your pants, or change your tights for sweats.

Notice the sensation.

Notice your lower back, does it feel like it needs to be stretched? do you need to fold yourself in half to see if it can loosen up or do you need to stretch your arms above your head? Be careful when doing this, you don't want to get air under your shoulder blades, that hurts!

Notice the sensation.

Notice your glutes, are you clinching your glutes because you're stressed and/or because the chair you're sitting on doesn't have enough cushion? Stretch, do a few squats.

Notice the sensation.

Notice your thighs, do they feel loose and relaxed? or are they slightly lifted off the chair in a manner where you feel the tendons behind your knees? Loosen up, shake them up a bit.

Notice the sensation.

Notice your knees, do you notice them more because you've started exercising, stretching, or not moving enough? Stand up, stretch them out if possible and sit back down.

Notice the sensation.

Notice your legs, do your calf muscles feel pressured? are you noticing the connection they have to the tendons behind your knees? Slowly stretch and listen to what they need. You know what to do next.

Notice your ankles, feet and toes, are they asking for you to take off your shoes because your toes and corns are hurting? or are your toes in need of being stretched because they've been in a shoe all day? wiggle them, stretch them with your hands, move them back and forth.

Notice.

Notice how you've been breathing as you've read through this, is your breath shallow? is it slow and steady? is it short and curt? do you need to take a long breath? Breathe in 1, 2, 3, 4 and breath out 1, 2,3,4. Breathe in 1, 2, 3, 4 and breathe out 1, 2,3,4. Breathe in 1, 2, 3, 4 and breathe out1, 2,3,4. Breathe in 1, 2, 3, 4 and breathe out 1, 2,3,4.

Now that you have noticed what's happening with your body, give your body what it needs in this very moment, water; a good stretch; a bathroom break; a nap, etc.

Notice if you are being hesitant in giving your body what it needs or if you're able to give yourself permission to meet your needs. When you allow yourself to respond to your needs by meeting them, you are teaching your body to trust your ability to take care of it. You are actively teaching your body to trust you.

YOUR PRESENT TRUST EXPERIENCE

TRUST to me means _____

_____

_____

_____ and I am/not able to say that I trust myself in how I engage and take up space in my world. The trust I have with myself directly impacts the trust I can extend to others, professionally, personally and intimately. In order for me to trust the people I've chosen, they have to _____

_____

_____

_____

and they have to show it by _____

_____

_____ in order for me to

trust that the decision I made about having them in my life

was the correct one.

The steps I take to decide on who I can trust and cannot trust

are _____

_____

_____

_____

_____

_____

_____and I take these steps as serious as I take

the steps to take care of me.

What I trust most about myself is _____

_____

_____because I practice and show consistency in my

_____

_____which allows me to feel

_____

_____

_____

_____

In my decision making and how I engage.

Notice if your answers are a reminder to what you already knew and somehow forgot, or if your answers feel and look different from what you imagined. Describe:

_____

_____

_____

In the following table, place your attention on every emotion mentioned and add your responses accordingly; give yourself permission to answer honestly

When I feel	1st Response	2nd Response
Joy		
Love		
Anger		
Sadness		
Secured		
Insecure		
Confident		

Review your responses and pause.

Notice what thoughts, memories, emotions and body sensations you experience as you read your responses out loud. Document your experience; you can write, draw, sing, react with whatever body movement you naturally want to make (squirm, smile, scream, move your shoulders, etc.)

_____

_____

_____

_____

_____

_____

When I feel	1st Response	2nd Response
Accomplished		
Challenged		
Disappointment		
Not knowing		
Unsafe		
Anxiety		
Failure		
Trust		

Review your responses and pause.

Notice what thoughts, memories, emotions and body sensations you experience as you read your responses out loud. Document your experience; you can write, draw, sing, react with whatever body movement you naturally want to make (squirm, smile, scream, move your shoulders, etc.)

_____

_____

_____

_____

_____

_____

_____

_____

Which responses and behaviors align with your current self?

_____

_____

_____

_____

_____

_____

_____

Which responses and behaviors no longer align with your current self?

_____

_____

_____

_____

_____

_____

_____

_____

What action steps do you want to start taking to be more aligned with your current self?

_____

_____

_____

_____

_____

_____

_____

_____

_____

Do you trust yourself to start taking those steps? _____ Yes _____ No

Trust is difficult because you have to believe that what you are experiencing is real and worthy of getting your attention. Your defenses and ego will get in the way, not allowing you to fully exercise your trust and emotional muscles. What you see, hear and taste does not always represent every aspect of the situation, but the feelings you experience can dictate whether you will respond or react to it, will it be your defenses, your ego, the story you made up in your head, or will it be your best and healthiest self that will respond. Trusting that your defenses will not abandon you in a time of survival, will allow you to be vulnerable, thoughtful, kind, empathic and compassionate with yourself and others, as you practice living. But if your fears and defenses kick in without asking for permission to take over, and without you noticing that they are in control, trust has gone out the window and you are in full defense mode. This can look like denial, frustration, anger, shame, numbing, fight, flight, freeze, etc.

As per Iyanla Vanzant in her book, "TRUST",

"Trusting yourself means having the confidence in yourself to do what is best for you, moment by moment. And if the choices and decisions you make do not work out for your highest good, you know and believe that you will be okay". (2015 P. 11)

It can't get more real than that, and more challenging.

Trusting yourself will allow you to take the time to respond and assess your experience before doing anything else. I ask you to put all your weaponry down, your machete, warrior sword, spears, knives and take your hunting, military, ninja gear off.

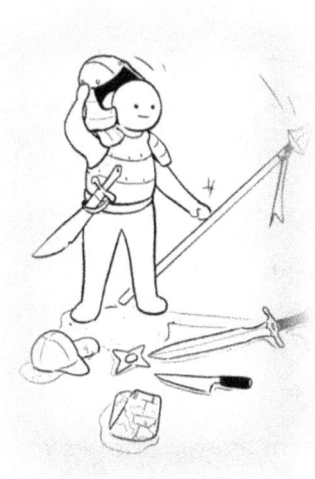

You will not be needing them in this journey. If they are needed, they will ask for your permission before slaying whoever you think needs it. They will ask ALL the questions needed to decide if there is danger or a crisis that requires their assistance.

I am fully aware that these defenses, your ability to trust yourself and others, are impacted by your gender, skin color, beliefs, societal norms and the stereotypes that have been placed on you.

The TRUST acronym can be utilized as a compass in your journey, it will need to be practiced in order for you to experience the changes you seek.

TRUST requires a level of safety within yourself. If you've experienced trauma, feeling safe can be very challenging, especially when you logically know there is no danger, but a part of your brain and body is screaming DANGER! DANGER. This means your brain and/or your body is stuck in the mix of the traumatic experience that happened and what is happening in the NOW.

Trauma takes away the feeling of safety, and to gain that feeling back or to learn to experience feeling safe enough, requires work and the skill of healing professionals. They can help you desensitize and reprocess those traumatic experiences, in order to allow your brain to store them as complete memories. If these memories are not desensitized, the loop and the fragments of something that happened, continue to get in the way of being curious and feeling safe.

This workbook may feel extra challenging, if you've experienced trauma. As you complete this workbook, notice your body experiences during prompts and when applying the exercises. If you notice patterns of behaviors that are not feeling right or are feeling a bit too off from what you think should happen, I ask that you seek support from a mental health professional, and ask to be assessed for Trauma. Trauma shows up in different ways, it can morph into other symptoms that may get confused for depression, anxiety, attention deficit disorder and other things that rationally make sense, until you dig just a bit deeper for the root cause.

If you are working with a mental health professional, I highly recommend that you inform them of the work you are doing in this workbook, it can be very helpful in your therapeutic experience.

As you learn to trust yourself and the decisions you make, you first need to be receptive to **TEACHING** yourself to respond to situations in a healthier manner then you may be accustomed to. You can identify how you want to be present in your relationships; how you want to take up space in this world, family, your community. It is necessary to practice these steps in everyday life whenever you can. Practice managing your emotions and behaviors with mindfulness, while you allow yourself to be reasonable and **RATIONAL** with yourself.

To become rational, you must acknowledge that you are attempting something new. There is a learning curve involved, so it will take time to adapt to the changes being implemented and to approach your expectations of yourself and others with rationality. I ask for your **UNDERSTANDING** that the same way there's a learning curve for you, there's a learning curve for your loved ones. The roles that you play in your relationships will shift and that impacts our ability to think rationally.

During this process, you must find safe spaces to feel secure. Be **SINCERE** with yourself, because as you adopt new behaviors full transparency will be needed. This will help you be mindful and to make healthier decisions. Begin by paying attention to your thoughts, you will see the shift in your thinking; you will become more intentional and thoughtful, allowing room to experience self-compassion, empathy and **TENDERNESS** with yourself and others. Remember, it's ok to experience discomfort, excitement, nervousness and all the emotions that will show up when trying something new.

Give yourself permission to walk through the experiences and call out judgments that may present themselves. Give yourself permission to ask for support during this TRUST process.

TRUST TOOLS IN ACTION

- **TEACHING**
- **RATIONAL**
- **UNDERSTANDING**
- **SINCERETY**
- **TENDERNESS**

TEACHING

The first step in the tools of TRUST is **Teach**; teaching your-self to unlearn behaviors that are no longer working for you; teaching yourself new behaviors that allow you to respond to your life situations, decisions, and life transitions in a healthy manner, from your adult, and wiser self. You will practice learning to differentiate between the defenses that are needed in the moment versus the defenses that you needed as a child growing up. Teaching yourself to trust your ability to protect yourself, without being impulsive in most or every situation.

Your defenses will always be with you, the question is whether you'll need them in every situation when feeling insecure, emotional, physically uncomfortable or when feeling vulnerable, shoot! when you're being human and doing what humans do, FEEL. Your defenses have been successful at protecting you, and you can teach them to differentiate between needing to step in NOW, LATER or NOT at all. If you feel all of your defenses are needed for your emotional, mental and physical survival in this moment, PAUSE!

Look around and notice the objects, colors, and smells in the room. Ask yourself, Am I safe in this very moment?

This simple pause teaches you that it's ok to stop, breath and to look around as you give yourself time to process. This tool can allow you to identify if the defenses are needed, and can get you to a place where you feel safe enough and able to take the steps you deem necessary. It also allows you to be and feel more in control. Notice if these defenses can assist you in trusting yourself. To be honest with you, they probably won't assist, because they need to feel useful.

> **Teach**: Practice, practice, practice! teaching yourself to naturally respond to your body's sensations, emotions and thoughts, in a healthy way. Do not minimize, judge, or shame your initial response. I ask you to embrace it and NOT avoid. By embracing you are teaching your body to trust that you will take care of it during challenges and times of uncertainty. The more you practice, the healthier you will respond and learn what your body is communicating to you. You will learn to distinguish between fear, intuition, and you knowing. This practice entails being vulnerable, open-minded, curious and **patient** with the adjustment period of

being a student of your body. This practice is incorporating the skill of patience.

The following questions can grant you clarity on how to apply this first tool.

How do you learn? _____

_____

What steps do you take to teach yourself something new?

_____

When you teach yourself something new, what do you experience?

_____

_____

_____

_____

_____

How do you practice patience during the learning process?

_____

_____

_____

_____

_____

In Pema Chödrön's book, "The places that scare you", it's shared that,

" *If we can practice when we're jealous, resentful, scornful, when we hate ourselves, then we are well trained". " Practice means not continuing to strengthen the habitual patterns that keep us trapped, doing anything we can to shake up and ventilate our self-justification and blame. We do our best to stay with the strong energy without acting out or repressing. As we do so, our habits become more porous".* (2018, p. 34)

Practicing allows you sooo many opportunities and grace to make mistakes, learn new skills and most importantly create the shifts you feel are necessary in this transformational journey.

Let's gain further clarity;

I can practice feeling _____
because it is the emotion and sensation that I
_____ and as I
acknowledge it, I can _____ and I will
_____

_____

_____

_____

Can you practice having compassion for the part of you that questions every decision you make and experiences uncertainty? ___ Yes ___ No Describe how:

_____

_____

_____

_____

_____

_____

_____

Can you practice curiosity about what you're experiencing when screaming at your kids to do something? ___Yes ___ No

What can that look like in real time?

_____

_____

_____

_____

_____

_____

_____

_____

Can you practice having compassion for the part of you that asks for everyone's opinions before making a decision? ____ Yes ____ No Describe how:

_____

_____

_____

_____

_____

_____

_____

_____

Can you practice allowing yourself to experience feelings of discomfort when practicing trust? ____ Yes ____ No. Describe how:

_____

_____

_____

_____

_____

_____

_____

_____

When I find myself fearing an emotion and/or allowing fear to guide me, I will _____ _____ which can allow me to calm my brain. I will identify the crisis and/or the life-threatening situation that is taking place, then I will

_____

_____

_____

_____

When feeling emotionally vulnerable, I will

_____

_____

_____

_____

The steps I will practice taking when I notice an overwhelming feeling will be (remember to not avoid, you want to practice responding)

_____

_____

_____

_____

_____

As you answered the questions, what did you experience? Were you honest with your answers or did you write down what sounded good and how you thought you should respond? __Yes __ No Describe _____

_____

_____

_____

_____

_____

_____

_____

_____

_____

How can you truly practice experiencing and not ignoring?_____

_____

_____

_____

_____

_____

_____

_____

If you found answering the questions difficult, you can practice by saying these phrases as you progress in this journey.

- This is challenging for me because it's something new and I don't know how to go about it, without making others feel uncomfortable. But it is ok for me to feel uncomfortable because it is something new and I will share this with _____ so they can be supportive in these moments.

- I am on the verge of getting burnt out and I want to get this project over with like I've always done, and then I'll schedule a massage. But I hear my body loud and clear, I will listen to it in this moment. I can give my mind some time to experience relief, get clarity and then I can continue with this project. This makes me feel uncomfortable and concerned about how my supervisor will respond, but if I don't take this time for me, I will break and will need to call out sick. I will inform my supervisor that I may need an extension in order to make this project a success. As I'm feeling the discomfort I will practice _____ and walk myself away from the ledge.

- I am so angry at myself for not saying what I really wanted to say, and now I am stuck with having to do _____ because I couldn't say No, I was too scared to. Now I am angry, annoyed, frustrated and stuck with this. What I can practice doing in this moment is _____

  _____

  __ and it allows me to change my mind, contact them back and say I cannot _____ and if I feel the need to give an explanation I will say

  _____

  _____ because it is true and it allows me to avoid lying to them and to myself.

- I need to make the decision to _____ and I normally contact _____ and _____ and _____ to hear what they think I should do, and this usually makes me feel _____.

  I can practice _____

  _____

  _____ and when I feel the discomfort and fear, I can _____ to calm myself down.

- I will practice making the following decisions by myself:

  _____

  _____

  _____

  _____

  _____

  And when I get the desire and/or feel the need to contact _____ I will stop myself and _____

As you completed the prompts and answered the questions, what was that experience like for you? What did you notice? Please describe, draw, color where in your body you felt the sensations and feelings.

THE PRACTICE OF BEING RATIONAL

$\rightarrow\!\!\!-\!\!\!-\!\!\!-\!\!\!-\!\!\!-\!\!\!\leftarrow$

RATIONAL

The Rational stage, allows you to check in, to practice being mindful of what you are experiencing, and aware of your surroundings in the situation. This tool has to be practiced, in order for your body and mind to listen and respond in a healthy manner. In this step, bring to mind the feelings or actions that challenge you having a rational response. For example; feeling angry, the euphoric feeling of love, lust, fears, excitement, jealousy; to think rationally and have common sense when experiencing these heightened emotions can be a hard ask. You will challenge the irrational reaction by practicing shifting your thinking, and a way to do this is by **slowing down, breathe and scan the room**. This can allow you to experience your emotions from a more informed space; in turn it gives you time to adjust and respond.

Be curious and flexible with the thoughts and feelings you are having. Trust that they are real whether you like them or not. Identify if these thoughts and emotions are yours or have been fed to you by society, family, culture, traumatic experiences, or the situation you are presently facing. During this rational process, beliefs about yourself impact how you treat yourself and your ability to decide if what you're experiencing is real.

This is an exercise I do with my clients; I ask them to verbalize what they are thinking, with no intention of understanding it or trying to make sense of it. Just say it how your brain is saying it. Clients tend to be hesitant because the good student in them makes them want to edit, censor it, make it sound nice, not be disrespectful, or try to have it make sense and resolve it before saying it out loud. I repeat it back to them in the same way they have shared it and ask for them to hear and feel what I'm saying. Then I ask them to repeat it, to notice the cadence in their voice and notice how their body is responding. There's usually a laugh, a cry, or an annoyance during this. This does not mean that they will miraculously be enlightened and change their ways, this is the start to curiosity, mindfulness, vulnerability, and the process to listening to themselves. I ask them to breathe and practice noticing. There's usually discomfort in the silence of it, but we practice trusting the silence and the important role it plays in how they learn to experience and listen.

Rational: Allow your brain the space to differentiate and decipher between the real and the made up, and decide from an informed space. What is fact? what is false? and what is logical? Recognize the process and the experience of learning. Notice your brain's creative skills, with its fixed beliefs and stories that can and will get in the way of your rational thinking.

Start this practice by asking yourself the following questions;

Do your feelings and self-questioning stem from old behaviors and defenses that aim to shield you from your past experiences and yucky emotions? If yes, please describe. _____

_____

_____

_____

_____

_____

As you practice self-trust, describe the past experiences that you are trying to protect yourself from

_____

_____

_____

_____

_____

Are you hesitant to trust yourself completely due to past emotions, fears of repeating the same mistake, or because of made up stories of what can happen in the future? Such as the what ifs. Please describe:

_____

_____

_____

_____

_____

_____

Are you hesitant to trust your decision making, because you fear being held

accountable? If yes, please describe what that looks and feels like for you

_____

_____

_____

_____

_____

_____

Distorted thoughts are very much based in the rational thinking of survival, or living in hostile places, or in seeking to control others due to fears and insecurities. Your rational thinking is influenced by your personal experiences, family, work environment, societal expectations, bias and discrimination. This leads to self- doubt and to questioning your abilities, it causes feeling irrational when trusting and honoring yourself or dealing with an inflated ego that is causing chaos in your relationships. Decision making can take place from a distorted place, based on how you look, where you live, stereotypes, and discrimination you've experienced or placed on others.

I want you to recognize the irrationality of not believing in your own experiences and emotions. Understand that you have grown up in an environment that encourages irrational behavior, where you are forced to suppress, ignore, protect and deceive yourself and others about what you're experiencing. As a result, your beliefs about yourself become distorted. I am asking you to challenge the naysayers and the dream snatchers, YEAP! Let's challenge them and the thoughts that accompany it. Are you going to allow them to stop you from taking rational steps? Probably, yes; because that's how you've been trained, but now you are practicing challenging it.

This is nuts, right? needing to practice trusting yourself without minimizing you, because THEY, the ones who you may or may not know, feel uncomfortable about their own s%$* and push that on to you.

Tips:

- Practice being aware and identify the behaviors that no longer benefit you.
- Observe and be curious about your experiences, desires, and genuine needs.
- Evaluate if they are realistic, rational, and supportive.

- Do not get fixated on one belief.
- Choose the behaviors you will practice changing because upholding them is irrational.
- Acknowledge your experience by verbalizing it and pausing as you process.

For example:

> I am feeling angry and frustrated, because I am saying one thing and sharing what I'm feeling, but no matter how I say it, they don't want to hear it or even try to understand it, because they say I don't really mean it or feel that way. This is definitely irrational and dismissive, I don't have to get caught up in their story, so I am going to step away and decide if this conversation is worth having.

> I have studied and learned this, I'm an out the box thinker, I go above and beyond and have been successful even when mistakes have been made. I speak up and advocate for myself, and in this situation, I know what I'm talking about, I have the proof, education and experience. But they need more proof, as if my long list of accomplishments is not enough and more than what they said they needed. This is unrealistic and

irrational. I will step away from what I want them to say, listen to what they are saying and then decide, if this is the right place for me.

I'm feeling anxious about these next steps. I should know what to do, even though I've never done it before. A bit irrational, but I have no time to get it together. I have to do it now and only have one chance, no room for error. But I understand that this is something new and will require research and further questioning, so I can understand what I am getting myself into before starting. Asking for support will save me time and energy in the long run.

I am annoyed and frustrated with a loved one because they said they would be here in 10 minutes and it's been 15. I know they are always late, but I just know something bad happened to them. They know I get anxious and start worrying about what bad thing can happen to them. I can reach out to them in 5 minutes to see if they've gotten caught up with anything else and may need more time, before I start creating stories. I will discuss setting healthy boundaries with them to address my stress before I begin to experience feelings of resentment.

What is your definition of rationality?_____

_____

_____

What does rational behavior and thinking look, sound and feel like? _____

_____

_____

_____

_____

_____

Listen as you speak and answer the following questions out loud.

Notice what you're experiencing and how I phrased it. (Many times, we believe that it is ok for others to experience emotions, but not for ourselves. We can be very harsh with ourselves). Be as honest as possible, and notice what you experience as you describe your answers and provide examples.

Do you think it's rational to believe that you have the right to feel emotions and make mistakes?

____ Yes ____ No

Describe what this looks and feels like

_____

_____

_____

_____

_____

Do you think it's rational to be compassionate and kind with yourself? ___Yes ___ No

Describe what this looks and feels like

_____

_____

_____

_____

_____

How do you approach being rational with yourself? Do these steps work?

_____

_____

_____

_____

_____

What changes would you like to make in order to rationally respond to difficult situations? (Difficult situations are not crisis, or life threatening, although it may feel like it is. We are referring to uncomfortable difficult and challenging situations that you do not want or like).

_____

_____

_____

_____

_____

_____

How will you practice applying those changes and differentiating between rational and irrational responses?

_____

_____

_____

_____

_____

_____

As you answered those questions, what did you notice? What was that experience like for you? Please describe, draw, color, etc.

THE PRACTICE OF UNDERSTANDING

UNDERSTANDING

It's imperative to **Understand** the importance of self-care on this trust journey. The main goal is to learn how to trust yourself by experiencing your emotions, recognizing the reasons behind them, and taking the time to understand why they happen. Understanding of self is key in learning to trust yourself, to trust your decisions, and to trust how you want to treat yourself and others. Understanding why you respond the way you respond, and being curious on the different ways you are able to be present for yourself and others, allows you to build the skills necessary to meet your goals.

Improving your skills will help you understand yourself better. This includes your unconscious thoughts, intentions, fears, wishes, wants, and needs. Going through this process may bring grief. You may experience loss of unmet expectations, challenge beliefs that never fit you, change values that never aligned with you, and change the dynamics of important relationships. Sadness in this process can lead to loneliness, isolation, and insecurity about your emotional and mental abilities. It's important to forgive yourself for past mistakes and beliefs. There were rational reasons for your past decisions and behavior, but you now have a choice in how you treat yourself.

Respect yourself and do not minimize your feelings or your experiences. You may think it's not a big deal, but your body doesn't, and will make it known now or later. Understanding allows you to fully practice applying the other steps, which focus on transparency, sincerity and kindness.

> **Understand**: Listen to understand what your need is, notice what it's asking of you. Practice patience to understand your behaviors by being curious and aware of how you normally respond to situations, and how you want to respond. Vulnerability is key in this step. As you practice compassion in the prompts below, try to

understand and clarify why you criticize and judge yourself. Welcome curiosity, it'll allow you to be receptive. (Curiosity arises from questions like why, what, how, and when.)

I understand that I was raised to believe and feel_____

and it caused me to _____

about myself, leading me to treat myself like

_____

I understand that the story that I am creating is based

on _____

and it's rational because _____

and irrational _____

and I can _____

I understand that I am afraid of _____

and this fear is getting in the way of _____

and it's causing me to feel _____

which leads me down the path of _____.

This feels like a lot for me, but if I don't do this for

myself, I will _____

_____

I understand the importance of expressing and having clear boundaries between myself and the people I choose to extend my trust to. These boundaries can be

_____

and sometimes it may feel uncomfortable to honor and express my boundaries because _____

_____

_____

_____

And when I experience this discomfort, I _____

_____

_____

I understand that this process is challenging, but I can continue to practice even when the situations look different with different people. But I know that I

_____

_____

_____ because I

can TRUST that I _____

while I still understand the fears I experience are

_____

_____ and I do not have to respond in the same way.

Curiosity about what you are feeling and experiencing, and understanding that you may not always find the answer, is OK. It is ok because you're acknowledging and practicing responding with more flexibility. You are being transparent, and this transparency allows you to learn and build confidence in your abilities.

In understanding yourself, you are practicing kindness, and empathy, as you challenge outside influences and messages that are not aligned with you.

For example:

I am feeling exhausted, not sleeping enough, burnt out at work and at home, but I have to keep up, because I can lose this opportunity or may be looked at as not caring enough or not being strong enough. But I understand that what I am doing in this moment is trying to push myself to do more when I need rest, my body is exhausted from trying to prove to others and myself that I can do everything. I understand why I'm feeling this way and why I am seeking to impress at my expense. This is not healthy for me or for what I am aiming to achieve. I get to choose...

> I have been scared of saying yes to this opportunity because I am not sure of what will happen after I say yes; it makes me feel vulnerable and uncomfortable. I understand that I'm feeling this way because it's something new and I am trying to protect myself, although at this time there is no danger. I can be fearful and hesitant and still say yes, because I am deserving of something good.

Sometimes you may want to dig your heels deep in the ground to prove to yourself that you are right, right in your impulsivity, assumptions, expectations, punishments, and testing of others. You may also believe that you will be taken advantage of, even with the understanding that it's unhealthy, or based on fear. This can look like:

> "I reacted that way because they didn't meet my expectations and didn't say what I wanted them to say. They don't care about me, so I am going to start ignoring them and see if they'll even care to notice. They should know better; they need to figure it out."

This response may sound familiar and quite common, but there is no understanding of the experience, or giving yourself the chance to be curious, to then respond. Curiosity in this scenario can look like this:

> Why am I feeling so upset? Did they say they didn't care about me? or do I feel like they don't care about me?

Another example;

> "I already said that I didn't care and that I was not going to do that, but I now want to. But I don't want to seem like a flip flopper that changes my mind, so even if they ask me multiple times to confirm, I have to say no, although I want to say yes. I can't back down now".

Curiosity in this scenario can look like this:

> How am I trying to be perceived by people who already know me? What is there to lose? Am I willing to miss out because of what they may think?

Respond to the following prompts and notice what you experience;

"I want to apply for this position at work, but I have not done enough projects to show that I deserve the position. I saw that so and so got a promotion and I did more than they did, but I'm different because I look like _____ and I speak like _____ and I need to still learn _____

_____ and once I do the extras, then they will not have a reason to say no, and I will be deemed qualified. But I know I'm capable, although I still won't know

_____

_____

_____ and they may use that as a reason to not give me the position. As I write this, I understand that the experience I have in _____ and all the work that I have put into learning new skills allows me to apply even if I feel _____ about this. I have the right to feel _____ because of what I have experienced in/with _____. In this moment, the rational decision would be _____

_____

_____

_____

_____

because what I am fearing _____ and I can trust myself to _____

So, I am going to take a breath, and take my next steps, because what I'm experiencing is understandable. It makes sense to want to avoid the feeling, but I am able to cope because I am an adult and I can speak with _____ because they are supportive, or I can _____

_____

_____

I am feeling anxious about sharing with my loved ones

_____

because it is not part of our traditions or cultural norms and/or it is not acceptable in our religion. These feelings of anxiety are causing me to _____

_____

_____ and feel _____

_____. I understand why I feel this way and why I would believe that they would respond _____

_____, but I do not have to respond with anxiety. I can _____

and I can ask _____for support because

_____

_____

_____which can allow me to feel less anxious.

What were these prompts like for you? Please describe, draw, color, etc.

THE PRACTICE OF SINCERITY

SINCERITY

In this process, transparency is necessary. You must be honest with yourself to build self-trust. Lying to yourself hinders learning to trust you. Avoid lying about your experiences, perceptions, self-esteem and about the mistakes you make. In this step, it's imperative to take your mask off, to acknowledge what you're feeling, and to verbalize how you feel about you, even if it sounds ugly. There is no room for perfectionism in this muddy process or anywhere as a human. Perfectionism will feed insecurities and expand the lack of trust in self. Mistakes are a part of the human experience, and learning to overcome them is part of your expansion process. In the children's book, " How to take the ACHE out of Mistakes by Kimberly Feltes Taylor & Eric Braun;

> *"give yourself a break when you naturally make mistakes going after goals and challenging yourself. What you should really fear is never making a mistake. Because then your brain never gets the "mistake" chance to become stronger." (2019 P. 103)*

Not making mistakes stunts your curiosity and growing process. Can you imagine how boring it would be? there would be no room for true innovation.

Sincerity in this journey is challenging, vulnerable, and humbling, but it grants you great strength, insight, maturity, and flexibility. I was raised to be strong and to follow through by any means necessary. I think the by any means necessary was created by what I witnessed and learned outside of my home. As a black Puerto Rican educated woman, which growing up I didn't know that was a big THING, it became an even a bigger thing as I got older. Leading me to believe that I will do whatever it took to accomplish my goals; especially when my ancestors had persevered through even tougher situations. If I committed to something, I would push myself to finish it, even if it no longer aligned with my needs or desires. I would deceive myself about the importance of completing the task, make assumptions about how others would perceive me, and rely on my "I'm a STRONG woman" belief to see it through. These perceptions, both self-imposed and imposed by others, seemed to match my personality. I kept my struggles and projects to myself, which only reinforced the distorted belief. The confidence I developed and proof of my ability to solve problems and achieve whatever goals I set, hindered my honesty with myself. The self-talk sounded something like this,

> "I complete everything I start or choose to do, NO MATTER WHAT".

This belief felt and sounded good to me, but it was causing havoc in my system. I use to promise myself,

> "I will not take on any projects for the next few years, until I fully complete this certification program and have fully digested the work, or until I am financially "stable" to take another project on."

Well, uum that promise to myself was an epic FAIL! for many years. The worse part about it is that I paid the price for it several times, until I had to be honest with myself and literally STOP.

Listen to this one,

I worked full-time as an Addictions and Substance Abuse counselor for an outpatient program at a hospital in Brooklyn, NY. I was a full-time graduate student, doing my internship, buying my first home, buying my first car, dating and going out with my friends, while saving money and preparing for my next projects, simultaneously. What the heck (%$^&) ? was I thinking.

You know what ended up happening?

I had a breakdown at work. I walked into my director's office and told her,

Me: I can't move my neck and can barely lift my shoulders; my entire body feels stiff. This came out of nowhere.

She was well aware of what I had been doing and she had warned me a couple of times of what could happen. She herself had experienced something similar.

Director: You are having a breakdown, go to the emergency room now.

I had to walk myself to the emergency department a couple of miles away, remember I worked at the outpatient program; getting on the 2 train, or taking the bus was not an option. I believed the pot holes and the sudden stops would make me scream. I was experiencing so much pain.

I slowly walked ZZZZzzzzzzzz

The never-ending walk. In the emergency room they provided me with muscle relaxers and took me out of work for 2 weeks.

My initial thought was: In a couple of days, I can go back to work, I have these groups to facilitate at work and at my internship. I need my internship hours and I have to complete this school work.

Once again, What the heck (%$^&)?

By some divine intervention, I decided to follow the doctors' orders, and I swore that I would not do that again. Well folks, it happened one more time, about a decade later. During that decade, I was still hard and semi lying to myself, well, lying to myself, SMH. It caught up to me, and this go round it wasn't as "bad" (can you still hear the denial at some level). I did end up going to the doctor; they did some testing and blood work, everything was "fine", no medications were needed this time. Meanwhile my entire body was covered in hives, including my eyes!

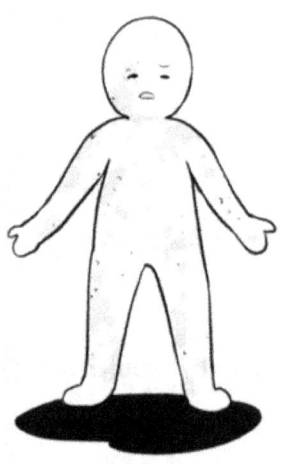

Doctor: what you've been up to?

I shared my version of the story

Me: Well, what's been happening is that I just purchased my home, I'm still paying the mortgage of my first home, it hasn't sold yet, so I now have two mortgages. I'm overseeing the outpatient and inpatient programs at the hospital, building my business, and trying to have surgery before I transition to being self-employed. I'm also exiting a relationship.

Doctor: That sounds like a lot, very stressful. As she gave me the wide eye look

Me: it's not too bad. Why is this happening?

She gave me THAT look, the look of stop it and listen.

Doctor: This looks and sounds like stress. Slow it down.

I listened and STOPPED.

Throughout this time, I believed I was being rational and understanding. I still had a breakdown. My brain reverted to old behaviors that no longer aligned with who I was becoming. **My rational thinking was skewed because of the positive results I was getting. I was not practicing self-compassion. Pay attention to the tricks your brain will play, leading you back to old habits that no longer suit you.**

It is still very difficult to trust that I can take the foot off the gas pedal, depend on my skills and my personality structure, but I've placed parameters and healthy boundaries with my projects; the strong woman beliefs, the I have to get this done NOW narratives, are challenged, and quieted, although they can still get very loud. Although these boundaries are hard to uphold, I work hard every single day to uphold them. Honesty holds me accountable and allows me to honor my boundaries with myself. I am very much able to set boundaries outside myself and to honor my No with others, but somehow, that No to me by me, whew! It's very challenging, especially when I know I can do it. I must trust that what my body is communicating is true, if not, then another breakdown is inevitable.

A breakdown at this age is not a wise decision.

Being sincere helps you recognize your inner thoughts and the beliefs that hinder you to trust and challenge your insecurities. It will allow you to practice understanding your experiences, as you see your raw self, and practice being accountable for what you're experiencing and your responses to it.

> **Sincerity:** Be honest about your true feelings and beliefs; verbalize the story that your brain is creating or the story that you have been told about yourself. Welcome your true self with mistakes, failures, fears, and challenges without self-punishment. Yes, this is going to be challenging. True honesty of what you need, acknowledgment of how you truly want to fulfill your needs and/or who you want to fulfill them is important. Differentiating between your true needs and

what you have been taught to believe you need by movies, all forms of media, from what you've witnessed in your home and in your community, etc. can be puzzling. Authenticity is not easy.

This step allows you to practice recognizing how you feel about yourself, and if you're willing to manage or teach yourself to manage your emotions, expectations, thoughts, and the stories you tell yourself. Here you will identify the steps you can take to practice being free of the expectations that have been placed on you, or you've created based on your experiences. Take the mask off and welcome the true self with mistakes, failures, fears, and challenges without punishing yourself.

Let's try it.

I don't trust my ability to feel my emotions of _____

_____

_____ and the thoughts that cause me to

_____ because it makes

me feel _____ ,

and when I experience these feelings, the memories that

come up are _____

_____

_____

_____

_____and   those

memories lead me to _____

_____.

As I acknowledge these thoughts and emotions, I am feeling

_____

_____

and I can practice allowing myself to _____

because   I   am   practicing   trusting   my   ability   to

_____

_____

Admitting to emotions that we dislike, or make us feel vulnerable is challenging. Just because they're challenging doesn't mean that you stop experiencing them. Admitting to feeling disappointed by someone we highly admire, or admitting to feeling scared, is a hard one to admit and acknowledge. I ask that you allow yourself to be fully transparent in the following prompts, notice the experience, notice how your brain may try to sway you away from the feelings and challenge the impulse to avoid; allow yourself to complete the exercise.

I am fearful of learning _____

when practicing _____

because the fear I experience stems from _____

and it makes me want to _____.

As I'm practicing being honest with myself, I am

experiencing _____

and the best way for me to respond to this in this very

moment is _____.

I find myself seeking guidance from _____

and when I look at them as a person and how I want them

to impact me I think/feel _____

_____. When I

pay attention to their behaviors and how they respond to life

situations and how I respond to them, I notice _____

_____

_____. I have found myself admiring who they

are/putting them on a pedestal because _____.

And I think that grants them access to _____.

The role they have always played in my life has been _____

_____

_____

_____

and I want them to continue/not continue playing this role because _____

_____

_____

Notice what you're experiencing, draw, color, journal.

Many times, we admire people for their ability to survive and for what they've been able to overcome; not noticing what those hurdles have been and how those hurdles impact who they are and how they view the world. Notice if you are seeking guidance from people who are fearful, in survival mode, overcompensating, or living from a space of scarcity. Pay attention to what you are expecting from them and if it's the right expectation, the correct role for who they are and for what you need.

FYI: *Your loved one's roles may need to be reassigned to a more fitting role. Role reassignment doesn't mean that you love them any less, it means that you are able to see them, and the role they play in your life needs to shift.*

This step comes with grief, loss, anger, relief, clarity, accountability, and acknowledgment of the role you play in each situation. Are you acknowledging your intentions? Are you doing it for yourself or for others? Are you lying to protect yourself or others? Are you avoiding and blaming others for your actions? This step can feel ugly and hard.

Let's be honest!

Remember the supports you identified in the beginning. It is important to seek their support because you may recall memories, and overwhelming feelings during this process. These tools will further clarify the role of important love ones in your life and can change the lens from which you have viewed them, which can cause this process to at times feel confusing, isolating, fearful and empowering with the greatest act of self-love.

The challenge of trusting your ability to cope with yourself and your human experiences will bring all types of discomforts. The need to seek approval or acceptance of your emotions from others will decrease with your TRUST tools. It helps you understand what is normal and provides an understanding of why and how you feel and act the way you do. You are holding yourself accountable for your feelings while practicing self-compassion. You are no longer hiding or lying to yourself.

Listen to your thoughts as you finish the following prompts.

If I teach myself to experience, slow down, quiet the noise and listen to understand my emotions and what my body is experiencing, I fear _____ and this fear gets in the way of _____

I've been avoiding acknowledging the fear of _____

_____

because I do not know what will happen if I continue to feel this way. When I think about what I'm fearing I feel

_____ and I

don't like it, so I _____

causing me to _____

_____

_____

In this very moment I can sincerely say that I will

_____ whenever I

experience this fear again. I understand that this will be a challenge for me and that I will make mistakes, but I will try my best.

I give myself permission to teach myself _____

because it can allow me to _____

and with that I can challenge the fears by _____

and it can allow me to become more _____

in my ability to trust myself.

When I feel insecure, I behave and think__ _____

and that leads me to _____

causing me to respond to my emotions and to what I'm

experiencing with _____

_____

At times it can lead me to try to fit in because I don't trust

_____

and this makes me feel _____

about myself. I understand that I do this because I

_____ and in this journey I will

give myself permission to _____

when I notice that I am trying to fit in and/or people please.

If I do not honor what I say I will do when these moments

arise, I will _____ and forgive

myself by _____

I want my life to look like _____

because _____

_____

but the reality is _____

_____

and that makes me feel _____.

I want to have people believe _____

because it makes me feel _____

and that means _____.

My unedited, uncensored, true beliefs about myself are

_____

Read that last prompt out loud.

Again, read the last prompt out loud.

Now read it out loud again and notice and identify the most important part.

What's the most important part? _____

How often do you allow those key words to guide you in your decision making and in your engagement with others?

_____

_____

Is this belief about yourself true? ____ Yes ____ No. Describe:

_____

_____

_____

_____

_____

_____

What steps do you take to uphold this belief?

_____

_____

_____

_____

_____

_____

Is this belief fair to you and your journey? ____ Yes ____ No

Describe:

_____

_____

_____

_____

_____

_____

Notice, document/draw what you're presently feeling, the sensations you're having in your body

THE PRACTICE OF TENDERNESS

TENDERNESS

During this process, I ask for your understanding of your human experience. Accept that as a human, you will make mistakes and decisions that may or may not benefit you. Remember, you're doing the best you can in those moments. Practice stepping into yourself by putting yourself first, acknowledging that you matter, getting curious about your discomforts as you're gaining awareness of your experience, and moving forward with compassion, kindness, and vulnerability as you trust yourself.

Doesn't that sound nice?

I am recommending that you practice feeling your feels on a daily basis. Every opportunity you see, practice trusting yourself; Starting with the simplest things, such as getting water when you feel parched, going to the restroom when you need to, stopping a conversation when you need clarity. You will slowly build on the more complex things that cause you heightened levels of discomforts, anxiety, bad memories, difficult relationships, etc.

Let's welcome the last step, Tenderness.

Tenderness involves welcoming vulnerability with self.

If you are not able to practice being kind and self- compassionate, the work you are doing gets impacted, your ability to process traumatic, challenging and important events gets stunted, the body work and breath work gets distorted. I am constantly reminding clients to be kind. Let's be tender, let's look at the part of you that is asking for support and in need of being seen and heard, and let's allow this part to learn to trust that you can take care of it. Tenderness can grant access to different parts of you that are experiencing fear, needing attention, and that are trying to people please, avoid, and numb. In this part of the work where insecurities, distortions, fears, anxiety, depression get heightened, with tenderness, we can slowly step in, be a bit more curious and even bold.

> **Tenderness:** Practice Self-compassion; practice tenderness the way you would with a baby, a puppy, a baby chick. Self-compassion will help you build your strength, trust and patience in your human experience. Forgiveness is a part of this process. Exercising these emotional muscles, allows room for a more positive perspective to shine through and support you in this journey.

Do you talk to yourself with loving words and actions? ___ Yes ___ No. Describe _____

_____

_____

How can you treat yourself with the same kindness you show others? And what does that look like?_____

_____

_____

_____

If you are having difficulties with answering that question or noticing what that looks like, try this:

Who are you the nicest to? _____

What about them makes you be so nice and kind to them? _____

_____

What about them makes you want to be kind and helpful? _____

_____

_____

_____

Are you worthy of viewing yourself in the same manner? (I know when we bring in the phrase self-worth, it makes some people squirm, and others instantly get defensive. I ask for you to be sincere with yourself and take notice of your behavior, and your responses to others, as you answer this question. Be vulnerable, say it, own it and then work at it).

___ Yes ___ No. Describe

_____

_____

_____

_____

_____

_____

Welcome your emotions and those loud thoughts by voicing them, so they can calm themselves down enough for you to hear and respond with the wisdom you have.

When I find myself being hard on myself for making a mistake, I normally _____

_____ but I can

_____

in order to _____

_____

When I need to make a decision and I find myself seeking feedback from _____

I will practice _____

_____

_____

and instead of _____ I will
practice being kind with myself by

_____

_____

When I notice that I need to share something challenging
with someone else, I tend to treat myself like _____

_____

_____

_____

and I will practice doing _____

_____

When I am low in motivation, I usually tell myself _____

_____

and that helps/doesn't help me because _____

_____

and I will continue/not continue doing that because _____

_____.

But by practicing tenderness, I will/ can _____

_____

_____

_____

_____

_____

I am hardest on myself when _____

_____

_____

_____

_____

and being tender with myself will make me _____

_____

_____

_____

_____

and I am open to practicing it because I can practice trusting

_____

_____

_____

_____

_____

We now welcome forgiveness into this process, and boooyyy is it tricky and challenging;

> I forgive, but I don't forget and will not let you forget either. Although I already said I forgive you and I forgive myself for allowing me to be such a fool for believing…

> I forgive myself for making a mistake, but all the new decisions I make, I can't stop thinking about that mistake. I become so fearful and annoyed, that it delays, and/or negatively impacts my decision making and how I feel about myself

Do those statements sound familiar? Is there a freak out moment taking place?

When others make mistakes that require forgiveness, are you able to forgive them? __Yes __ No Have you ever forgiven yourself for mistakes you've made? And I am not referring to the type of forgiveness where you are seeking to be accepted, and/or forgiveness based on fear because you may get punished by God or go to hell or something of sorts. I'm referring to forgiveness for past mistakes, and not shaming or judging yourself for those mistakes anymore. I'm referring to the forgiveness for a mistake you've made or someone else has made, where you have created healthy boundaries and have been able to move onward in the relationship (if it's worthy and safe) and with your decision making.

You can start practicing forgiving yourself by using these prompts. This will help you trust yourself in future situations.

I forgive myself for choosing to _____

with _____, because in that moment I felt

the best thing for me to do was to _____

and even though I felt uncomfortable with myself and the

situation, I still chose to _____

because I did not want the other person to feel _____,

say _____, or judge me by

_____. Forgiving myself

for those actions is difficult, but I am choosing to practice

being worthy of making mistakes because I am human and

worthy of having emotions such as discomfort, not

knowing, feeling guilty, annoyed, sad, because I deserve to

_____

I am practicing forgiving myself for that situation, because it

is going to allow me to _____

and I have learned that when I am feeling _____

and/or when I am thinking _____,

I am not able to make decisions as a whole person. The

decisions I make come from a place of _____

and not so much from a rational, logical place. So, from now

on, I can practice feeling my emotions and not making a

decision until I've _____

_____

I can utilize the POWER of being **Present, Observing** my experiences, practicing my **Worth** as I **Explore** my options and **Resolve** situations.

Sometimes the stories/statements that I tell myself to punish myself for a past act, or decision are _____

_____

Moving forward:

- I will practice verbalizing my story, and noticing if it's based in reality or if it's being made up because of my past experiences.

- I will practice differentiating between making a decision based on avoiding that others feel bad, and/or that I will be judged.

- I will practice being true to myself and to honor my values. With the understanding that mistakes will definitely take place, and that I can practice trusting my ability to respond and cope with situations in real time without punishing myself.

- I will practice _____

_____

_____

_____

Some of the experiences you will have, can show up with somatic symptoms (Body sensations, tensions; responses that may initially have no words) other things that can show up that you may be more familiar with can be: Anxiety, depression, fear, loud criticism of self-and/or others, negative self-talk, etc.

When you practice forgiveness. Ask yourself how you want to manage and respond to the sensations and emotions you will experience. Identify the steps you will begin to practice taking with empathy, self-compassion, and trust within yourself and your abilities.

What steps are you going to take to practice applying what has been covered in this section?

Step 1:

Step 2:

Step 3:

Step 4:

Step 5:

As you completed this exercise, I ask that you notice what the experience was like for you; you can draw, write, collage your experience.

Books that you can read to further dive into the journey of forgiveness are:

"The book of Forgiving" by Desmond Tutu; and "Forgiveness 21 Days to Forgive Everyone for Everything" by Iyanla Vanzant. Remember that not everyone will respond to forgiveness in the same way, and the forgiveness experience is yours. It does not mean that you forget, it means you get the opportunity to learn.

What are you presently experiencing ? _____

_____

_____

Trust yourself to hear the part of you that is most present at this time and be curious about what it's seeking to fulfill. Give yourself a few minutes. Notice what you're feeling, sensing, thinking, as you give yourself time to process, and to gain a further understanding of you in this very moment.

What's coming up for you now? _____

_____

_____

_____

_____

_____

How do you want to respond to yourself in this very moment? Describe _____

_____

_____

_____

_____

_____

Being kind to yourself can challenge wanting to punish yourself for mistakes made, or for the opportunities you feel you may have missed. Tenderness allows room for you to truly trust yourself and to continue practicing how you respond to you.

TRUST IN REAL LIFE SITUATIONS

Exercise:

Using the emotions, behaviors, thoughts, and sensations list with the dining table image, identify a situation, (a decision, fear, emotional experience/ vulnerable situation) that is making you doubt your ability to make a decision, to put yourself first, set a boundary, to express your needs, or to practice self-care.

It could be anything

For example:

- Sharing something important with a loved one that makes you feel vulnerable.

- Applying for a new position
- Building a new relationship
- Setting boundaries with family
- Experiencing discomfort
- Practicing being in silence
- Parenting a toddler, teenager, adult
- Choosing to leave

Choose anything that feels doable to you in this moment and you will gradually practice on the more challenging ones later.

Practice applying your TRUST tools. Notice what you experience as you apply the tools in real time in real situations.

The decision to trust yourself is represented by the table. The chairs around the table are your TRUST tools. Additional chairs are the emotions, thoughts, sensations, and other factors that either support or not support your goal of trusting yourself and decision making. Many times, these factors, thoughts, emotions will take a seat on the side and may need to be addressed at the main table because they be loud.

Example:

I am avoiding feeling angry and frustrated because I have been working hard on maintaining order in this project/home and I am not appreciated or even acknowledged. When I feel this way, I avoid by going shopping, eating, saying that it's ok, and being passive aggressive, because if I allow myself to feel these feelings, I don't know what pandora's box I will be opening, and it's best for me to just avoid it. I feel tension in my shoulders, neck, chest.

Utilizing TRUST tools;

Decision to make: Should I experience my emotions

The situation: Avoiding my real emotions because of fear that I will lose it and I don't like the feels.

Teaching: Practice acknowledging: I am feeling **angry, discomfort** and **frustrated** because I am not being listened to, and it's making me feel very stressed, uncared for. I know if I say something I'm going to cry and I have been feeling so stressed that **I'm not sure** if I will be able to stop crying. **I'm going to feel my feelings.**

Rational: I am feeling stressed because I have been doing a lot lately, taking on a lot of projects, trying to maintain the house, trying to support my family like I'm supposed to do, trying to fit everything into my schedule. The last time I shared what I was feeling and thinking, it turned out to be a bad day, I was harshly judged because of my decision, although it was the best thing for me.

Understanding: I am feeling **angry** because I know how this makes me feel, it happens often, but **I don't know** how to respond. I don't like this feeling, and **I wish** someone else would step in. I have a reason to feel **sad** and to want to protect myself and not feel, but I acknowledge and understand why I'm feeling this way.

Sincerity: **NOPE** I do not want to feel these emotions, what are they going to say about me? I'm **fearful** of being judge. I don't want them saying that I don't have everything together, that I'm not strong enough. I need support, I need relief, I need affection and I am afraid of asking for it.

Tenderness: I have the right to feel this way, **it's ok** for me to fear how it's going to be received. I will not overeat this time and I will feel my feelings, be angry without punishing myself. I will allow myself to cry, so I can release this tension that I am feeling. **It's ok** for me to feel all of this, even when I've been told I always have to be nice and that I **should** always have it all together, but in this moment I do not. I will breathe to calm down and I will choose how to respond once I'm feeling better.

Emotions, Behaviors, Thoughts, Sensations List

Teaching	Rational	Understanding	Sincerity	Tender
Rational	Judgment	Anger	Sadness	Fear
Joy	Hesitation	Apprehension	Shame	Insecurity
Love	Courage	Trust	Worthy	I need to ask others
I'm not sure	Wisdom	Avoidance	Numbing	Rage
I'm not enough	I can't say that	I'm not allowed	What are they going to say?	How am I going to be judged?
I'm going to be isolated	No one is going to speak to me	I don't like how this feel	I need someone to stand in	I'm not making this decision
I just can't	I can try this	NOPE	Keeping my mouth shut	I have autonomy to
It's ok	I'm going to be ok	I'm allowed to	I should	I shouldn't
I can	It's fair	Why me?	I don't want to	What if
I wish	I want to, but	I am going to do this	Discomfort	Weird
Tension	Stress	Annoyed	WTF	I'm just being Needy

I know	I knew	I want	I need	I will
It's a Sin	The last time	I was raised to	Need to Protect	Maybe later
My belief	My faith	My religion	My church	My gender
My role	I feel Guilty	I owe	Punishment	My Culture
My parents	My family	My friends	Tradition	I need Control
Confused	Conflicted	Resentment	Tension in chest	Back pains
Headache	Achy throat	Tension in neck	Tension in shoulders	Tension
Fulfilled	Clumsy	Silly		

To be continued

You learn that it's okay to be human when you allow yourself to experience your emotions.

What are your thoughts on that statement?

_____

You can handle and own your experience because every emotion you feel is valid.

What are your thoughts on that statement?

_____

Acknowledge and understand the messages and expectations directed at you. Understand and respect the impact these messages have on your feelings, your desires, your identity, your thoughts. Express yourself and let your body feel the relief of not suppressing or censoring your emotions because of how it may look. Avoid numbing and avoiding, because it allows you to gain trust in your ability to handle your emotions without sacrificing your autonomy, mental, physical health, and humanity.

Continue practicing TRUST, add your flavors to it; acknowledge the experience and the expectations you are placing on yourself, notice whose voice it is, and choose if it's worth it. Be patient with yourself during this journey. This is a practice. Use the following as a guide when making decisions based on TRUST and challenging situations that require more thought.

Decision to be made _____

Loudest emotions _____

Realistic Options with no judgments or people pleasing:

_____

_____

_____

_____

Solution _____

_____

_____

_____

What did this feel like?

_____

_____

_____

_____

_____

What does trust mean to you now?

_____

_____

_____

_____

_____

_____

_____

With this fresh lens: Do you trust yourself when allowing people in your world? ___Yes ____No Explain.

(For example: When choosing a partner; when choosing friends; when choosing to assist, when you choose to apply for a new position or asking for a promotion or for more money)

_____

_____

_____

_____

_____

_____

_____

_____

How does it look and feel when you trust yourself? How does it look and feel when you do not trust yourself? What do you experience?

_____

_____

_____

_____

_____

_____

_____

How can you determine whether to trust yourself or others? Do you use instinct; prior experiences; what you grew up believing in; etc. to guide you in this decision. What do these steps look like? Describe

_____

_____

_____

_____

_____

_____

_____

Can you practice trusting you? ____ Yes ____ No Describe

_____

_____

_____

_____

_____

_____

_____

_____

The awareness that I have gained and allowed myself to experience is allowing me...

_____

_____

_____

_____

_____

_____

_____

_____

_____

The story that I told myself when I started this workbook was (how did pressures show up; did creative adjustments play a role)

_____

_____

_____

_____

_____

The experience I allowed myself to have during this process was?

_____

_____

_____

_____

_____

The story that is real and present now is

_____

_____

_____

_____

_____

The action steps I can continue taking are

_____

_____

_____

_____

_____

The trust that I have in myself will allow me to

_____

_____

_____

_____

_____

I will redo this workbook on Month_____ Day _____Year _____

Congratulations on completing this workbook. By following its suggestions, you have started to understand yourself and develop self-trust. Understanding yourself will boost your decision-making, self-treatment, abilities, needs, and expectations. Be intentional, recognize your accomplishments and put what you've learned into practice.

REFERENCES

Author, Iyanla Vanzant (2015). *TRUST; Mastering the four essential trusts.* U.S Hayhouse Inc.

Author, Pema Chödrön (2018). *The places that scare you; A guide to Fearlessness in Difficult Times.* U.S: Shambhala Publications Inc

Author, Dr. Brené Brown (2012) *Daring Greatly How the courage to be vulnerable transforms the way we live, love, parent and lead.* U.S: Gotham Books

Author, Kimberly Feltes Taylor., & Author, Eric Braun Illustrator: Steve Mark (2019) *How to take the ACHE out of Mistakes.* U.S: Free Spirit